MW01601242

Property of

See more books at www.AnnetteWoodGraphics.com

Made in the USA
Columbia, SC
14 November 2023

26164451R00062